AI-POWERED DATA PRIVACY COMPLIANCE & DATA PROTECTION FOR SMALL BUSINESSES

SABIRA AREFIN

AI Powered Data Privacy & Data Protection For Small Businesses

February 2024

Genre: Privacy & Online Safety

Published by

INOVIE BOOKS

Available worldwide

Visit us at:

www.inoviebooks.com

GRATITUDE

This book would not have been possible without the unwavering support and inspiration of several incredible individuals.

First and foremost, my deepest gratitude goes to my husband, Ashfaq Rahman. His expertise in the field of AI, Machine Learning, and Natural Language Processing was an invaluable resource throughout the writing process. His constant encouragement and insightful feedback fueled my determination and helped shape this book into its final form.

To my dear friend, Farjana Sikder, your support has been immeasurable. Sharing your deep insights and developers' perspective and expertise as an AI software design engineer at Microsoft was essential in enriching the content and ensuring its accuracy. I cherish the cozy fall evenings spent discussing this project with you and your husband Safwan Khan in your beautiful home. Farjana & Safwan your friendship and positive influence have played a significant role. Your work as an AI cloud security engineer adds another layer of expertise to the circle of support that made this book possible. Together, we dreamed of not only protecting our children from the online world but also sharing our knowledge with others through publications and presentations. I am grateful for your unwavering encouragement and belief in this endeavour.

This book is a testament to the power of collaboration, friendship, and shared dreams. Thank you, Ashfaq, Farjana, and Safwan, for being a part of this journey. Your contributions have made a world of difference.

Sabira Arefin

Sabira Arefin
February 2024

CONTENTS

INTRODUCTION

In the modern era of technology, data is frequently likened to the new oil, serving as a vital resource for numerous businesses and governments, influencing their decision-making, fostering innovation, and enhancing efficiency. Nevertheless, the growing dependence on data has underscored the crucial concerns of safeguarding data privacy and security. As data breaches and cyberattacks continue to escalate, there is an urgent demand for strong measures to protect data. This book will delve into the role of Artificial Intelligence (AI) in tackling the issues of data privacy and security.

In the digital age, data is the lifeblood of any business, but for small businesses, it can also feel like a double-edged sword. While customer information fuels marketing campaigns and personalizes experiences, it also comes with a growing burden: ensuring data privacy and security compliance. Navigating the labyrinthine world of regulations and best practices can feel like steering a dinghy through a legal squall, with each new law or amendment another wave threatening to capsize operations. Fines, reputational damage, and lost customer trust are the very real perils lurking beneath the surface.

Data governance plays a critical role in safeguarding personal information online. With the vast number of websites and search engines, it's necessary to have proper measures in place to ensure data privacy. Using secure sharing tools can also enhance the protection of personal information. The rise of data breaches and privacy violations means individuals and businesses should be vigilant in managing their digital presence on their company websites. This includes safeguarding their personal data, communities, and online data. Data governance violations can have severe impacts, not only on individuals' privacy but also on the reputation and trust of communities, companies, and organizations. As more organizations and service providers undergo digital transformation and rely on digital marketing strategies, understanding how to protect data privacy is crucial for search engines and other service providers.

From the information collected through websites and cookies to third-party access to personal data, there is a wide range of potential vulnerabilities that need attention in digital privacy and security. Ensuring the safety of personal data has become increasingly important as search engines and digital marketing continue to play a significant role in our online lives. In the age of digital transformation, individuals, organizations, and service providers must take proactive measures to navigate the complex digital marketing landscape successfully. By prioritizing digital security and implementing robust privacy practices, organizations can ensure the safety of sensitive information on their website. This is essential for maintaining a trustworthy online presence and being easily discoverable by search engines. Additionally, providing a secure service is crucial for building trust with users.

But amidst this churning chaos, a beacon of hope emerges from artificial intelligence (AI). No longer confined to science fiction, AI is transforming the compliance landscape, offering small businesses a lifeline and turning data protection from a daunting chore into a proactive advantage. This is not just about ticking regulatory boxes; it's about building trust, fostering brand loyalty, and unlocking the true potential of your data. So, let's dive deeper into the compliance conundrum faced by small businesses and discover how AI can be the game-changer that steers your enterprise towards a secure and prosperous future.

CHAPTER ONE

UNDERSTANDING DATA COMPLIANCE & PRIVACY

Understanding data compliance and privacy is crucial for small businesses navigating the ever-changing digital landscape. It involves adhering to regulations and best practices to protect sensitive customer information and maintain trust. Here's a comprehensive overview:

Data Compliance: Data compliance refers to meeting legal and regulatory requirements related to data handling, storage, and processing. Small businesses must comply with various laws and regulations, such as the General Data Protection Regulation (GDPR) in the European Union, the California Consumer Privacy Act (CCPA) in the United States, and industry-specific regulations.

Data Privacy: Data privacy focuses on protecting individuals' personal information from unauthorized access, use, or disclosure. It involves implementing measures to safeguard sensitive data, such as customer names, addresses, financial information, and health records. Privacy policies and procedures should be clearly communicated to customers to build trust and transparency.

Organizations can navigate shifting data privacy legislation by adopting transparent data practices that comply with the regulations. This involves being upfront about using cookies and providing clear information to users. By openly communicating how they collect, store, and use customer data, companies can establish trust with their customers. It's also essential to be transparent about the use of cookies. Transparency in data mapping and cookies allows consumers to comprehend what information is being collected from them and how it will be used.

However, navigating data privacy regulations isn't always easy. Organizations must balance meeting business needs with addressing customer privacy concerns, including data mapping and cookies. While businesses rely on consumer data, including cookies, for purposes such as targeted advertising or improving the user experience, they must do so in a way that respects individual privacy rights.

To achieve this balance, organizations can implement robust data protection measures such as encryption, access controls, regular security audits, and cookies. These measures help safeguard customer information while allowing businesses to leverage valuable insights from the data they collect, including cookies.

Key Considerations for Small Businesses:

Data Collection and Storage:

Collect only the necessary customer data and store it securely.

Implement access controls and encryption to protect sensitive information.

Data Processing and Usage:

Use customer data only for the intended purposes and obtain consent when necessary.

Regularly review and update data processing practices.

Data Breaches and Incident Response:

Have a plan in place to respond to data breaches and notify affected individuals promptly.

Conduct regular security audits and employee training.

Third-Party Data Sharing:

Carefully select and monitor third-party vendors who handle customer data.

Ensure that data-sharing agreements are in place.

Data Retention and Disposal:

Determine appropriate data retention periods and securely dispose of outdated information.

Implications for Small Businesses:

The implications of non-compliance with these regulations are significant, encompassing legal repercussions, financial penalties, and damage to reputation. Small businesses must navigate these complex frameworks to ensure they meet the requisite standards and build trust with their customers.

Defining Common Data Security Threats:

Understanding data compliance involves acknowledging and mitigating potential threats. Small businesses often face challenges such as:

Cybersecurity Attacks: Ranging from phishing to ransomware, cybersecurity threats constantly evolve. Small businesses, often lacking robust defenses, become prime targets.

Insider Threats: Employee negligence or malicious intent can lead to data breaches. Implementing strict access controls and employee training is crucial.

Third-Party Risks: Collaborating with vendors introduces additional vulnerabilities. Small businesses must scrutinize their partners' security measures to prevent data leaks.

International Data Transfers

Cross-Border Data Flow Challenges: With data and technology becoming increasingly global, reconciling different privacy standards across jurisdictions is challenging. Laws like GDPR, LGPD, and CCPA take varied approaches, making international data transfers complex to ensure continuous compliance.

Role of AI in Facilitating Transfers: AI can help bridge regulatory gaps by automating data mapping, auditing transfers for legal bases, and documenting processing. Tools may translate consent policies between regions and flag regional access or use restrictions. This eases friction from varied privacy laws.

Ensuring Protection Abroad: However, simply transferring data does not ensure continuous protection—the receiving parties must maintain an adequate level of privacy. AI can monitor downstream processing and recommend remediation if foreign handlers fail to uphold promised standards. Cross-border flows require vigilant oversight.

Harmonizing Global Frameworks: Ultimately, greater international agreement on core privacy principles and interoperable legal mechanisms through standards bodies may be needed. AI can analyse regulations across jurisdictions to highlight divergences hampering digital trade and suggest pathways to progressively harmonized global privacy frameworks.

In the dynamic landscape of data compliance and privacy, small businesses can navigate these challenges by staying informed, adopting robust security measures, and leveraging technology solutions that simplify the complexities of regulatory adherence. This proactive approach not only safeguards sensitive information but also positions small businesses as trustworthy stewards of data in an increasingly interconnected world.

CHAPTER **TWO**

INTRODUCING THE AI COMPLIANCE ASSISTANT: YOUR GUARDIAN ANGEL IN THE DATA MAZE

In the ever-evolving digital landscape, navigating the treacherous waters of data privacy and security can feel like steering a sailboat through a hurricane of regulations and threats. For small businesses, particularly, the sheer complexity of compliance requirements can be overwhelming, leaving many feelings lost and vulnerable. But fear not, fellow entrepreneurs, for a beacon of hope shines on the horizon: the AI Compliance Assistant.

This revolutionary tool, no larger than a widget but wielding the power of cutting-edge artificial intelligence, acts as your guardian angel in the data maze. Imagine a tireless sentinel, constantly monitoring your every step, ensuring you remain on the straight and narrow path of compliance. Let's delve deeper into how this marvel of technology works and empowers your business to thrive in the age of data-driven trust.

Integration at the Point of Sale: Seamless and Discreet

Picture this: a customer completes a purchase at your online store. As the payment information flows through your system, the AI Compliance Assistant, seamlessly integrated with your payment point, springs into action. It's like having a microscopic compliance inspector embedded within your digital infrastructure, analyzing every byte of data with lightning speed.

Algorithmic Eye: Scrutinizing Practices with Precision

But the AI Assistant is far more than a mere observer. It wields a sophisticated arsenal of algorithms, trained on the intricate nuances of various data privacy regulations like GDPR and CCPA. These algorithms meticulously scan your data collection practices, comparing them against the relevant regulatory frameworks. Like a skilled detective, the AI uncovers any potential discrepancies, highlighting areas where your data handling might fall short of compliance standards.

Beyond Scrutiny: Automated Verification for Guaranteed Trust

Compliance isn't just about passive adherence; it's about actively building trust with your customers. The

AI Assistant understands this critical principle. It automates the verification of your Terms and Conditions (T&C) agreements. Imagine customers seamlessly clicking "Agree" to clear, concise, and regulation-compliant T&Cs, instantly establishing a transparent and trustworthy relationship. No more legalese-laden documents or confusing opt-in forms; the AI Assistant ensures crystal-clear communication, empowering your customers with informed consent.

Reaping the Rewards: A Wealth of Benefits for Your Business

The benefits of embracing the AI Compliance Assistant extend far beyond simply avoiding hefty fines and regulatory headaches. Let's explore the tangible advantages this technological champion brings to your small business:

Reduced Risk of Non-Compliance: The AI Assistant acts as your proactive shield, constantly identifying and mitigating potential compliance issues before they snowball into costly problems. With its watchful eye, you can rest assured that your data handling practices are consistently on the right side of the law.

Enhanced Customer Trust and Brand Reputation: In today's data-driven world, transparency and responsible data stewardship are paramount for building customer trust. The AI Assistant, by guaranteeing clear communication and compliant data practices, strengthens your brand image and fosters lasting customer loyalty.

Improved Data Governance and Operational Efficiency: The AI Assistant doesn't just identify problems; it offers solutions. It guides you towards implementing best practices for data governance, streamlining your data handling processes, and optimizing your operational efficiency. Imagine reducing manual compliance tasks and dedicating your valuable resources to core business activities.

Gaining a Competitive Edge: In a market where data privacy is a differentiator, the AI Assistant sets you apart from the competition. By showcasing your commitment to responsible data handling, you attract tech-savvy customers who value their privacy and demand transparency.

Investing in the Future: A Wise Choice for Growth

The AI Compliance Assistant is not just a tool; it's an investment in your business's future. It empowers you to navigate the ever-changing landscape of data privacy with confidence, freeing you to focus on what matters most: growth and success. Remember, in the data-driven economy, trust is the new currency, and the AI Assistant helps you mint it every day.

Reg-Tech Partnerships

Reg-Tech refers to the use of emerging technologies like artificial intelligence, machine learning, cloud computing and other innovations to help firms address regulatory challenges and compliance requirements more efficiently and effectively.

Reg-Tech Opportunities

The rapidly growing Reg-Tech industry consists of startups and software vendors developing innovative solutions to help organizations address changing compliance and reporting needs. Emerging Reg-Tech companies offer specialized tools and services around monitoring regulatory changes, conducting risk assessments, automating routine reporting tasks, and streamlining other compliance processes. This allows compliance teams to focus on higher-value work. As the compliance landscape grows increasingly complex with more regulations and greater expectations for risk management, relying solely on internal resources is challenging for most companies. AI systems, with their ability to ingest and intelligently analyse vast amounts of data, can partner with Reg-Tech firms to enhance the scope and depth of support provided to clients. Through integration, AI and Reg-Tech can work together to offer end-to-end governance solutions that help lower costs and improve outcomes for regulated businesses across industry sectors.

Enhanced Risk Identification

Reg-Tech companies employ teams of policy and legal experts that continuously monitor global regulatory authorities for any updates or changes to rules. They also track media and litigation reports that could indicate emerging compliance issues. By integrating with these Reg-Tech partners, AI assistants are able to ingest a wider range of structured and unstructured data related to the evolving regulatory environment. This enhances their natural language processing and machine learning models over time. The assistants can then leverage this expanded knowledge graph to conduct more comprehensive risk assessments for clients and proactively flag potential gaps or underserved risk areas where new capabilities may need to be developed. Such risk identification becomes more robust through the network effects of Reg-Tech collaboration, ensuring clients remain aware of and prepared for risks on the shifting compliance horizon.

Streamlined Processes

By tightly integrating with Reg-Tech software platforms and directly connecting to their workflows and application programming interfaces, AI assistants can seamlessly automate many routine yet time-intensive compliance tasks. Through this collaboration, the assistants can help with activities like populating required fields in periodic reports, pulling together supporting documents for audits, generating standardized responses to regulatory inquiries, and outlining remediation plans when issues are identified. This level of end-to-end process automation enabled by Reg-Tech partnerships transforms what were once highly manual, administrative tasks into a smooth, optimized flow. The AI assistant takes the work out of the hands of overburdened compliance analysts, freeing them up to refocus their expertise on more complex strategic analysis, risk assessments, and policy guidance that better leverage their high-level skills. The result is a streamlined, efficient approach to governance that multiplies a compliance program's resources and impact.

Improved Response Times

While AI systems excel at automating routine matters based on their extensive training, novel or complex compliance questions and situations still require human expertise. Through collaboration with Reg-Tech partners, AI assistants have an invaluable backup of experienced compliance professionals to draw from when faced with queries or edge cases outside their existing knowledge. Whether it's a regulation in a new jurisdiction, an uncommon transaction type, or an industry-specific nuance, the AI can instantly escalate these unfamiliar matters to its Reg-Tech connections. Drawing from their network of subject matter experts around the globe and 24/7 availability, Reg-Tech firms ensure the AI assistant receives timely guidance to resolve compliance dilemmas. This allows the AI to respond promptly to its clients without delays, further streamlining the resolution of issues. The expertise resource sharing between AI and Reg-Tech partnerships amplifies both capabilities, to the ultimate benefit of joint customers.

Data and Insights Sharing

AI and Reg-Tech partnerships are mutually beneficial relationships where both parties share valuable data and insights to reinforce a continuous feedback loop of learning and innovation. Reg-Tech platforms provide the AI assistant access to their vast pools of regulatory documents, compliance reports, risk assessments, and other data to enrich its knowledge. In exchange, the AI system supplies its Reg-Tech partners with aggregated insights gleaned from its interactions with a wide network of clients. With permission, it shares benchmarks, emerging trends, compliance patterns, and other analytics. Over time, as this reciprocal data and insights sharing strengthens their collaboration, AI and Reg-Tech offerings become tightly integrated into comprehensive one-stop solutions. Regulated organizations are then empowered with a full suite of advanced governance tools tailored to their unique needs. The collective intelligence of AI and Reg-Tech alliances drives the entire compliance industry forward.

CHAPTER THREE

CONSUMER GUARANTEES AND MERCHANT RESPONSIBILITIES

In the dynamic landscape of online transactions, striking a balance between business interests and consumer rights is paramount. Merchants play a pivotal role in ensuring that data collected at transaction points is handled responsibly and ethically. This chapter explores the expectations for merchants, underscores the significance of transparent data terms and conditions, and proposes a model for a mutual agreement between consumers and merchants to uphold data privacy.

Expectations for Merchants When Collecting Data:

In the digital age, where data is a valuable currency, merchants bear a crucial responsibility when collecting consumer information. The following expectations set the foundation for ethical and compliant data practices:

Informed Consent: Merchants must obtain explicit and informed consent from consumers before collecting any personal information. This involves communicating the purpose of data collection and seeking permission.

Limited Data Collection: Merchants should collect only the data necessary for the transaction. Unnecessary information increases the risk of data breaches and may infringe on consumer privacy.

Secure Storage: Implement robust security measures to ensure the safe storage of collected data. This includes encryption, access controls, and regular security audits to identify and address vulnerabilities.

Data Minimization: Adopt a policy of data minimization, where only essential information is collected. This not only reduces the risk of data misuse but also aligns with privacy principles.

Transparency: Provide clear and accessible information about the merchant's data practices, including how the data will be used, stored, and shared. Transparency builds trust and empowers consumers to make informed choices.

Regular Compliance Audits: Conduct regular audits to ensure ongoing compliance with data protection regulations. This proactive approach helps identify and rectify potential issues before they escalate.

Transparent Data Terms and Conditions

Transparent data terms and conditions form the bedrock of a trustworthy relationship between merchants and consumers. The clarity and comprehensibility of these terms are essential to building consumer confidence and fostering a transparent digital marketplace.

Plain Language: Express data terms and conditions in clear and simple language, avoiding jargon that might confuse consumers. This ensures that individuals can easily understand how their data will be handled.

Accessibility: Make data terms and conditions easily accessible to consumers. This information should be prominently displayed on the merchant's website, especially during the transaction process, to allow consumers to make informed decisions.

Notifying Changes: If there are updates or changes to data terms and conditions, notify consumers promptly. Changes should only be implemented after obtaining renewed consent from users.

Education Initiatives: Consider implementing educational initiatives to help consumers understand the importance of data privacy. This could include informative content on the website or email campaigns emphasizing the merchant's commitment to safeguarding customer data.

Model for Mutual Agreement between Consumers and Merchants

To establish a harmonious relationship between consumers and merchants regarding data privacy, a model for mutual agreement can be implemented.

This agreement ensures that both parties are aligned on how personal data is handled and provides a framework for ethical and transparent practices.

Elements of Mutual Agreement:

Scope of Data Usage: Clearly define the scope of data usage, specifying the purposes for which the data will be utilized by the merchant. This could include order processing, personalized marketing, or analytics.

Data Retention Period: Outline the duration for which the merchant will retain the consumer's data. Be transparent about the reasons for data retention and the mechanisms for secure disposal after the specified period.

Third-Party Sharing: If the merchant intends to share data with third parties, disclose this information in the mutual agreement. Specify the types of third parties involved and the purpose of such sharing.

Consumer Rights: Acknowledge and affirm the rights of consumers regarding their data. This includes the right to access, rectify, and, if necessary, delete their personal information.

Security Measures: Detail the security measures in place to protect consumer data. This could involve encryption, secure servers, and routine security audits to instil confidence in consumers.

Consent Mechanism

Opt-In Mechanism: Implement an opt-in mechanism for data collection, ensuring that consumers actively agree to share their information. This can be achieved through checkboxes or clear calls to action during the transaction process.

Granular Consent: Allow consumers to provide granular consent, enabling them to choose the specific types of data they are comfortable sharing. This empowers users with control over their personal information.

Periodic Review and Renewal

Regular Reviews: Conduct periodic reviews of the mutual agreement to ensure its continued relevance and alignment with evolving business practices and consumer expectations.

Renewal of Consent: Establish a process for renewing consumer consent at reasonable intervals. This ensures that consumers are continually aware of and comfortable with the data practices of the merchant.

Enforcement and Accountability

Complaint Resolution: Outline a transparent process for resolving consumer complaints regarding data privacy concerns. Provide clear channels for consumers to voice their concerns and receive timely responses.

Accountability Measures: Establish accountability measures for the merchant in the event of a data breach or non-compliance with the mutual agreement. This could include remediation actions and, in severe cases, legal consequences.

Consent and Preference Management

- **Consent Management**

Obtaining and documenting clear consumer consent for data collection and usage practices is crucial for compliance. AI assistants excel at streamlining the consent process through personalized notifications and straightforward preference menus presented during account creation and service enrollment. Consumers can thus efficiently provide granular consent for each proposed data activity upfront. The assistant then assumes responsibility for centrally managing an individualized consent record for every user, continuously verifying that only consented-to data processing occurs. It also handles periodic consent renewal reminders to ensure preferences stay current. By automating complex consent workflows and enforcing documented consent on an ongoing basis, AI helps ensure business activities remain properly authorized according to each user's preferences.

- **Preference Enforcement**

Once users designate how their data may be utilized through a robust preference-setting dashboard, AI assists with actively applying these customized rules. It restricts data access or proposed uses that have not received the individual's approval. The assistant monitors in real-time for any attempted violations of recorded preferences from internal or third-party systems. Through uniform enforcement of preferences across internal tools and external integrations, AI helps provide users with assurance and transparency around how their information truly is and is not being used. Any potential compliance gaps around honouring end-user control can swiftly be remediated. AI strengthens an organization's capability to guarantee customers maintain self-determined dominion over their personal data.

In Summary, the framework proposed for ethical data practices includes expectations for merchants, emphasis on transparent data terms and conditions, and a model for mutual agreement. This framework is comprehensive and aims to safeguard consumer privacy, as well as establish trust and cooperation in the digital marketplace. As merchants navigate the complexities of data collection, responsible handling of consumer information becomes a strategic imperative for sustainable business growth, rather than just a legal obligation.

CHAPTER FOUR

HARNESSING YOUR AI GUARDIAN: A STEP-BY-STEP GUIDE TO UTILIZING THE COMPLIANCE ASSISTANT

The digital landscape constantly shifts, and data privacy regulations follow suit. For small businesses, navigating this ever-evolving terrain can feel like trekking through a dense forest without a map. But fear not, intrepid entrepreneurs! You now have a trusty companion on your journey: the AI Compliance Assistant. This revolutionary tool, packed with cutting-edge intelligence, is designed to simplify compliance and empower you to handle data responsibly. Let's delve into a step-by-step guide that unveils the full potential of your AI guardian angel.

Step 1: A Seamless Onboarding - Integrating the AI Widget

Think of integrating the AI widget as inviting a helpful friend into your online store. The process is designed to be smooth and effortless, requiring minimal technical expertise. Simply follow these steps:

Connect with your platform: Identify compatible payment platforms and follow the intuitive setup instructions provided by your AI Assistant vendor.

Enter your store details: Provide basic information about your business, such as its name, location, and industry. This helps the Assistant understand your specific context.

Choose your regulations: Select the relevant data privacy regulations your business adheres to, like GDPR, CCPA, or others based on your region and customer base.

With these simple steps, your AI sentinel is now firmly embedded in your digital infrastructure, ready to meticulously oversee your data handling practices.

Step 2: Customizing Your Shield - Configuring Compliance Parameters

Think of this step as tailoring your compliance shield to match your unique needs. Each regulation comes with its own set of requirements, and the AI Assistant allows you to configure them precisely:

Data collection parameters: Specify the types of data you collect from customers, their purpose, and the legal basis for the collection. This ensures every data point aligns with regulatory frameworks.

Storage and retention limits: Define how long you store customer data and implement procedures for secure deletion once the retention period expires.

User consent management: Configure the options for customers to provide clear and informed consent for data collection and usage, complying with regulations like GDPR's "right to be forgotten."

Data breach notification settings: Establish protocols for promptly notifying authorities and affected individuals in the case of a data breach.

Remember, customization is key. By diligently outlining your specific compliance parameters, you empower the AI Assistant to become a highly personalized guardian for your data practices.

Step 3: Real-time Vigilance - Monitoring and Reporting for Peace of Mind

Now, imagine your AI Assistant as a tireless sentinel, constantly monitoring your data collection activities like a watchful hawk. Its sophisticated algorithms scan every data interaction in realtime, comparing them against your configured parameters and relevant regulations. If any potential discrepancies arise, you'll receive immediate alerts:

Compliance risk notifications: The Assistant immediately flags any concerns related to data collection, storage, or usage that deviate from your chosen regulations.

Detailed reports: Dive deeper with comprehensive reports highlighting specific areas requiring attention, providing valuable insights into potential non-compliance issues.

Proactive guidance: The Assistant doesn't just identify problems; it suggests corrective actions and best practices to address them swiftly, ensuring you stay on the right side of compliance.

With real-time monitoring and insightful reporting, you gain peace of mind and the ability to address compliance concerns before they snowball into bigger problems.

Step 4: Turning Insights into Action - Refining Data Handling Practices

Your AI Assistant is not just a compliance watchdog; it's a data guru in disguise. Its comprehensive reports offer valuable insights that go beyond regulatory adherence:

Data minimization: Analyze reports to identify unnecessary data collection and implement practices to collect only the information you genuinely need.

Data security optimization: Utilize insights to strengthen your data security measures, such as access controls and encryption, proactively minimizing the risk of breaches.

Operational efficiency: Identify areas where data handling processes can be streamlined, reducing manual tasks and freeing up resources for other business activities.

Data Privacy Engineering

Privacy by Design

Privacy by Design is an essential principle for building trust and embedding compliance into organizational systems and operations. It requires proactively considering data protection implications throughout the entire lifecycle of products, services, and technologies - from the initial conceptualization phase through iterative development, full implementation, and eventual retirement. At each step, Privacy by Design mandates comprehensively assessing how personal information will be collected, used, shared, and retained, then engineering robust technical and policy-based controls to address potential risks to individual privacy. Controls are purposefully designed to make privacy-supportive options the easiest default choices for both organizations and individuals. Privacy is thereby systemically reinforced as a guiding principle intrinsic to - rather than separable from - how a company conducts business. When faithfully applied, Privacy by Design fosters a privacy-centric organizational culture and translates broad commitments to data stewardship into tangible safeguards encoded directly into technologies, product features, vendor agreements, staff training protocols, and other everyday operations. This helps ensure privacy protections keep pace with innovations.

Implementing Foundational Practices

To effectively embed its privacy principles into practice, a company should carefully consider a core set of foundational measures. This involves collecting only data that is strictly necessary to enable the product or service functionality being provided, and avoiding excessive data collection "just in case" it may prove useful later. Where possible, anonymization techniques should be leveraged to further de-identify personal information and manage risks. Strict retention limitations enforce the timely deletion or anonymization of data once it has served its originally intended purpose. Strong access controls through techniques like encryption, access logging, and authorization rules help enforce "need to know" based on user roles.

Designing intuitive privacy control interfaces and impact assessments also helps ensure individuals fully understand and consent to how their data is being used while addressing ethical obligations. Such privacy engineering aims to simultaneously establish accountability over process compliance while facilitating innovation through responsible uses of personal data that enhance product experiences over the long run. With foresight and technical safeguards built on foundational practices, companies can develop new offerings while navigating legal and ethical requirements with confidence.

By continuously refining your data handling practices based on the Assistant's guidance, you achieve optimal data governance and operational efficiency, creating a win-win situation for both compliance and your business.

CHAPTER FIVE

NAVIGATING THE VALUE SPECTRUM: FREE VS. PAID VERSIONS OF YOUR AI COMPLIANCE ASSISTANT

In the ever-evolving landscape of data privacy, where regulations shift and customer expectations rise, choosing the right compliance solution is crucial for small businesses. While the AI Compliance Assistant empowers you with its core functionalities, understanding the differences between the free and paid versions unlocks the full potential of its value proposition. Let's embark on a deep dive into both options, guiding you towards the perfect fit for your specific needs and budget.

The Free Version: Your Compliance Foundation

Think of the free version as a sturdy starting point on your compliance journey. It equips you with essential tools to navigate the data privacy landscape:

Basic compliance monitoring: Stay informed about potential violations of core regulations like GDPR and CCPA through real-time alerts.

Fundamental data insights: Gain basic insights into your data collection practices, identifying areas for improvement within your chosen regulations.

Access to key resources: Benefit from educational materials, FAQs, and community forums to deepen your understanding of data privacy best practices.

Ideal for:

Small businesses with limited data collection: If you handle minimal customer data, the free version provides a solid foundation for basic compliance.

New businesses testing the waters: For startups still establishing their data handling practices, the free version offers a risk-free trial run of the AI Assistant's capabilities.

The Paid Version: Your Compliance Powerhouse

Upgrade to the paid version and unlock an expanded arsenal of features that propel your compliance efforts to new heights:

Advanced compliance coverage: Extend your compliance shield to encompass a wider range of complex regulations specific to your industry or region.

In-depth analytics and reporting: Gain granular insights into your data practices with detailed reports, data visualizations, and customizable dashboards.

Automated T&C verification and consent management: Ensure seamless customer consent, streamline processes, and reduce manual tasks.

Priority support and exclusive features: Enjoy faster response times, dedicated account managers, and access to cutting-edge compliance tools.

Ideal for:

Growing businesses with increasing data volumes: As your customer base expands and data collection scales, the paid version offers robust compliance support.

Businesses operating in highly regulated industries: The advanced features ensure adherence to even the most intricate regulations.

Compliance - conscious businesses seeking optimization: If data privacy is a core value and operational efficiency is paramount, the paid version empowers you to excel.

Advantages of Data Access for AI Training and Improvement

Some may wonder about the data used by the AI Assistant and its impact on privacy. Rest assured, transparency and trust are our guiding principles:

Opt-in participation: Businesses choose to share their data for AI training and improvement with complete transparency and control.

Strict anonymization: All data undergoes rigorous anonymization processes, ensuring individual privacy is never compromised.

Purpose-driven usage: Data is solely used to enhance the accuracy and effectiveness of the AI Assistant, ultimately benefiting all users.

By opting into data sharing, you contribute to a collective effort to continuously improve the AI Assistant's ability to navigate the ever-changing regulatory landscape, benefiting all businesses seeking its protection.

Ensuring Transparency and Trust in Data Usage

You need to understand the importance of data privacy and should be committed to upholding the highest ethical standards:

Clear and concise privacy policies: Understand exactly how your data is collected, used, and protected through readily available documentation.

Regular security audits: You need to undergo independent security audits to ensure your systems are robust and data is safeguarded.

User control and deletion rights: You retain complete control over your data and can request its deletion at any time.

Investing in the paid version doesn't compromise your commitment to data privacy; it strengthens it by contributing to a more intelligent and effective AI Assistant, ultimately safeguarding your business and your customers' data.

Let's delve into it further.

Industry-Specifics:

E-commerce: Imagine a bustling online store, its digital shelves brimming with customer data. Here, the AI Assistant acts as a vigilant guardian, ensuring GDPR compliance for European customers while streamlining CCPA consent management for US buyers. There are countless examples of those online retailers who, while implementing the paid version, reduced compliance violations by 90%, saving over $20,000 in potential fines and boosting customer trust through transparent data practices.

Healthcare: In the sensitive world of healthcare, data privacy is paramount. The AI Assistant empowers clinics and hospitals to navigate HIPAA regulations effortlessly. Medical practice Dr. Joyce & Associates, for instance, leveraged the free version to identify and rectify data security vulnerabilities, avoiding a potential data breach and safeguarding patient privacy.

***Financial Services*:** Banks and financial institutions juggle complex regulations like The Payment Card

Industry Data Security Standard (PCI DSS) and The Federal Financial Institutions Examination Council (FFIEC). The AI Assistant becomes their trusted advisor, providing real-time monitoring and in-depth reporting. Leading banks leverage the paid version, achieving a 75% reduction in compliance audit time and freeing up resources for core banking activities.

Ensuring AI Safety through Guidelines and Standards

As AI technologies become more advanced and integrated into

various aspects of our daily lives and businesses, it is important to establish robust standards and policies to ensure these systems are developed and applied safely, ethically, and for the benefit of humanity. As AI capabilities continue to grow, there must be appropriate safeguards in place to prevent potential harm. Various reputable organizations like the OECD, IEEE, and EC have proposed comprehensive guidelines on important issues like algorithmic transparency, accountability for decisions, mitigating bias, ensuring privacy and security of sensitive data, and responsible development practices.

Adhering to established principles around these types of issues will be crucial for building public trust and the adoption of AI-powered tools. As AI systems are increasingly used to make meaningful decisions impacting individuals, following standards on transparency allows their decision-making processes and outcomes to be understood and potentially audited. Principles of accountability help assign responsibility for AI outcomes. Addressing issues like bias and unfair discrimination via algorithmic impact assessments helps protect vulnerable groups. For tools designed to process highly sensitive personal information, it will be especially important to demonstrate compliance with strong privacy and security laws and show that individuals' data and consent are protected.

The development of the AI Compliance Assistant, meant to automate important compliance work involving regulated data, has followed established guidelines on issues such as data minimization, purpose specification, security safeguards, individual consent and control, oversight throughout the system's lifecycle, and responsible practices. Adhering to principles from organizations focused on AI safety helps ensure the tool can be safely and responsibly integrated into compliance workflows without compromising important ethical standards or allowing potential harm. Ongoing oversight and evaluation against emerging standards will also be important as both AI and data privacy laws evolve over time. Prioritizing requirements for issues like transparency, accountability, fairness, and security helps build confidence in innovative tools and promote their safe, lawful, and ethical use.

Industry Hypothetical Case Studies

Financial Services Case Study

A large national bank implemented an AI assistant to help simplify and streamline its Sarbanes-Oxley financial reporting process. Plagued by manual paperwork and excess employee hours spent responding to reporting requests, the bank trained its AI using historical reporting documents and internal control frameworks. This allowed the assistant to begin generating narrative compliance responses automatically by pulling data from relevant source systems. Overnight, the AI eliminated 500 employee hours per quarter previously spent on reporting tasks. Additionally, its risk analytics capabilities were employed to continuously monitor for control deficiencies and intelligently guide internal audit prioritization, reducing related costs by 15% annually. Whereas SOX compliance once took six weeks of manual effort each cycle, the AI assistant now ensures controls are monitored around the clock and reporting is delivered seamlessly, on an ongoing basis.

Healthcare Case Study

A leading health insurance provider sought to bolster HIPAA compliance through the implementation of an AI assistant. With over 500,000 employees accessing tens of millions of confidential patients' records each year, the AI was designed to encrypt sensitive data and intelligently monitor user access patterns across the organization's network in real time. It autonomously issues alerts on any potential violations of access policies. The assistant also personalized an interactive online training program, dramatically improving completion rates from 50% to over 90% among staff. Further, through its consent management capabilities, the AI streamlined patient processes for authorizing data sharing according to their preferences. By gleaning insights from past incidents, the AI also informed infrastructure enhancements such as privileged user restrictions and cloud security configurations, closing pathways for potential privacy breaches.

In summary, some may wonder about the data the AI Assistant utilizes for its insights and training. We understand your concerns, and transparency is paramount. The Assistant operates on a strictly opt-in basis, and you have complete control over the data you share. Additionally, as explained earlier, all data is anonymized and used solely for improving the Assistant's accuracy and effectiveness. This symbiotic relationship ensures your trust and allows us to continuously refine the tool to better serve your compliance needs.

By embracing the AI Compliance Assistant, you unlock a world of benefits beyond mere compliance. You gain peace of mind, build customer trust, streamline operations, and ultimately pave the way for sustainable growth. So, take the first step and welcome your AI guardian angel into your online store. With its unwavering vigilance and insightful guidance, you can navigate the data maze with confidence, steering your business towards a future of trust, transparency, and success.

CHAPTER SIX

NAVIGATING THE FRONTIER: THE FUTURE OF AI - POWERED COMPLIANCE

The digital world is constantly changing, and regulations regarding data privacy are always evolving. Although the AI Compliance Assistant is a useful tool for navigating this complex landscape, there are even more exciting possibilities on the horizon. Let's explore the fascinating realm of AI-powered compliance, including emerging trends, the increasing use of AI across various industries, and the ethical considerations that guide responsible development.

Emerging Trends in AI for Data Privacy and Security:

AI could evolve from reactive monitoring to proactive guardianship. Here are the trends that shape the future.

Predictive Compliance: AI algorithms will analyze historical data and industry trends to predict potential compliance risks before they occur, enabling businesses to take preventive measures.

Privacy-enhancing Technologies (PETs): Techniques like federated learning and homomorphic encryption will allow AI to analyze data without compromising individual privacy, unlocking secure insights while upholding data protection.

Explainable AI (XAI): As AI models become more complex, XAI will provide interpretable outputs, allowing businesses to understand the reasoning behind compliance decisions and ensure fairness.

Continuous Adaptation: AI models will continuously learn and adapt to evolving regulations and data landscapes, ensuring businesses remain compliant without requiring constant manual updates.

The Potential for Broader Adoption Across Industries:

While the initial focus might be on highly regulated industries like finance and healthcare, the benefits of AI-powered compliance will extend far and wide:

Small and Medium-sized Businesses (SMBs): Affordable AI solutions will empower even smaller businesses to navigate complex regulations, levelling the playing field and fostering fair competition.

Non-profit Organizations: Data privacy is crucial for NGOs collecting sensitive information. AI can streamline compliance processes and free up resources for their core missions.

Supply Chains: Globalized supply chains pose complex data privacy challenges. AI can track data flows across the chain, ensuring compliance at every stage and building trust with consumers.

Building a Responsible and Ethical AI Ecosystem for Compliance:

As AI takes the helm of compliance, ethical considerations become paramount:

Algorithmic Bias: We must address potential biases in AI models to ensure fair and nondiscriminatory compliance practices.

Data Governance: Robust frameworks for data collection, storage, and usage are essential to prevent misuse and safeguard individual privacy.

Transparency and Explainability: Users must have a clear understanding of how AI makes compliance decisions, fostering trust and accountability.

Human-in-the-Loop Systems: While AI automates tasks, human oversight and judgment remain crucial to interpreting complex situations and ensuring ethical compliance.

By promoting candid conversations, encouraging collaboration among stakeholders, and upholding ethical principles, we can ensure that AI becomes a powerful force for good. This will guide businesses towards a future where responsible data handling and robust compliance are integral parts of their operations. As we move forward, we must remember that our ultimate goal is not just to achieve compliance, but to build trust, empower individuals, and create a sustainable digital ecosystem where privacy and innovation can thrive together.

AI Auditing and Explainability

Auditability of AI Systems: As AI becomes more integrated into compliance systems, there will need to be frameworks for auditing these systems to ensure proper functioning, detect biases, and build accountability. Auditing AI will involve testing models on diverse edge cases, observing outcomes over time, and examining decision logs and training data to validate performance. Regulators may require automated "self-checks" and issue audit certificates for high-risk tools.

Demand for Explainability: To maintain a human-over-the-loop approach and enable the challenging of automated outcomes, compliance AI systems will need to provide explanatory insights into their decision-making. Techniques like SHAP values. LIME and attribution summaries will be used to generate understandable rationales for triagers, investigators, and regulated users. This builds processes for identifying and addressing potential unfairness.

Importance of Interpretability: Transparent and interpretable models like linear models, decision trees, and fallback rule lists may become preferable to deep "black-box" architectures for sensitive compliance purposes, even at the cost of predictive accuracy. The trade-off favours accountability over pure efficiency, given the liabilities around technology-driven decisions affecting individuals and businesses.

Regulatory Standards for Auditing: Global standards bodies and data protection authorities will play a vital role in establishing common auditing frameworks, routine self-assessment procedures, and oversight of high-stakes systems. Ensuring robust and privacy-aware model governance through audits and explanations will be key to regulatory acceptance of autonomous compliance tools.

Data Anonymization and Synthetic Data

- **Data Anonymization**

Anonymization techniques play an important role in balancing privacy protections with beneficial data uses. The goal of these methods is to transform personal information so that individuals can no longer be reasonably linked to their data through re-identification. Common techniques include redaction of direct identifiers, aggregation of data elements to a less granular level, perturbation involving purposeful noise injection, and one-way hashing. When applied skillfully through a rigorous process, these alterations can strip connections to identity while retaining sufficient data quality and volume for tasks like model training. However, preventing re-identification also requires strong technical measures and policy controls due to persistent re-identification risks. Organizations must mitigate these risks through security safeguards, access restrictions, legal agreements, and rigorous oversight of any third-party sharing. Ensuring anonymization meets stringent standards of "irreversible de-identification" involves vetting by expert data protection officers. Their role is vital for validating appropriateness and conducting ongoing assessments to affirm the protection of individuals amid an environment of open data and emerging technologies.

- **Synthetic Data Generation**

Synthetic data holds promise as a privacy-preserving alternative to using real personal records without consent. Through sophisticated techniques such as generative adversarial networks, synthetic data algorithms can programmatically fabricate realistic proxy datasets that share statistical properties and patterns with authentic source data. These simulated datasets may contain synthetically derived individuals, entities, relationships, and attributes—but no actual person's data or identity. When implemented through privacy-aware differential techniques, synthetic data allows model training at massive scales unachievable by other methods, all without collecting or retaining a single individual's confidential information. This approaches the ideal of enabling data-driven innovation on representative information while eliminating privacy risks to people. Synthetic data therefore provides a solution that supports—both privacy rights and technological progress in a lawful, ethical manner.

Privacy Enhancing Computations

- **Homomorphic Encryption**

Homomorphic encryption introduces the ability to perform calculations on ciphertexts, or encrypted data, without first decrypting it. This opens up significant potential for privacy-preserving analytics. By leveraging the properties of certain encryption schemes, functions like addition, multiplication, and other operations can be directly applied to encrypted user records. Institutions can then leverage machine learning or other computational techniques to derive insights and patterns from the encrypted data corpus, all without the raw data ever being exposed in plaintext. While homomorphic encryption schemes remain computationally intensive, ongoing research continues to expand the types of functions that can be supported as well as boost efficiency. With the right cryptographic protocols and management of encryption keys, homomorphic encryption provides a promising avenue for data-driven discovery and personalized recommendations using sensitive health, financial, and other records—while fully maintaining confidentiality and access controls over the raw sources. As the field advances further, homomorphic encryption could help unlock valuable insights from privacy-restricted data in a lawful and ethical manner.

- **Multiparty Computation**

Multiparty computation introduces methods for multiple stakeholder organizations to jointly perform analyses over their private, distributed data holdings without pooling or exposing raw inputs. Through secure measures like secret sharing techniques and circuit encryption protocols, individual participating nodes can contribute encrypted fragments of their private datasets toward–collaborative computation. No single party learns the encryption keys needed to decrypt others' inputs or view full outputs alone. This enables privacy-preserving joint modelling scenarios, including integrated medical studies, predictive analytics drawing on financial and commercial records, and more. As MPC protocols are still computationally burdensome, ongoing research continues optimizing efficiency while upholding security and privacy guarantees. When further streamlined, MPC shows promise for enabling data-driven insights and partnerships among entities with legal, ethical, or competitive data-sharing restrictions.

CHAPTER SEVEN

BLOCKCHAIN FOR DATA PRIVACY AND MONETIZATION

In the ever-evolving digital landscape, data is often hailed as the new oil, a valuable resource with immense economic potential. However, the quest for data monetization has given rise to growing concerns about data privacy. This chapter explores the transformative potential of blockchain technology as a solution to harmonize the imperative of data monetization with the paramount need for data protection and privacy.

The Evolving Data Landscape

Recent years have witnessed a surge in data-driven technologies and innovative monetization models. This shift prompts a re-evaluation of how we perceive and manage personal information. Blockchain, initially conceived for cryptocurrencies, has emerged as a robust solution capable of reshaping the data landscape. It delves into various applications where blockchain can be leveraged to protect data privacy, even in scenarios where data is monetized.

The Dance Between Data Privacy and Monetization

The intricate dance between data privacy and monetization poses a significant challenge. Businesses aspire to harness the wealth of information they collect, while individuals demand control and protection over their personal data. Blockchain, renowned for its secure and transparent record-keeping, emerges as a potential game-changer in striking a delicate balance. This chapter explores the question of whether blockchain can genuinely safeguard data privacy while facilitating ethical and secure monetization.

Understanding the Data Dilemma:

At the heart of the issue lies the tension between two seemingly conflicting desires:

Individual Privacy: Users rightfully demand control over their data, fearing misuse, discrimination, and privacy violations.

***Data Monetization*:** Businesses see their collected data as an asset, aiming to leverage it for targeted advertising, personalized experiences, and revenue generation.

It's important to understand that blockchain technology can transform the way we perceive data privacy and monetization. The decentralized and unalterable ledger provided by blockchain ensures that data is safeguarded against unauthorized access and use. This aspect is particularly crucial for sensitive information, such as medical records or financial data.

Traditional approaches often leave data vulnerable to breaches, centralized control, and opaque monetization practices. Blockchain offers a unique solution to these issues.

Blockchain: A Glimpse into a Secure and Transparent Future:

Imagine a distributed ledger, accessible to all participants yet tamper-proof, where data is stored securely and transparently. This is the essence of blockchain, a technology characterized by:

***Decentralization*:** Data is not stored in a single location, eliminating the risk of centralized breaches and unauthorized access.

Immutability: Once recorded, data cannot be altered or deleted, ensuring trust and data integrity.

***Transparency*:** All participants can view and verify transactions, fostering accountability and reducing information asymmetry.

In addition, blockchain can also be used to enable data monetization. By allowing individuals to control who has access to their data and how it is used, blockchain can create new opportunities for individuals to generate revenue from their data. For example, individuals could sell their data to researchers or businesses for use in market research or product development.

Smart Contracts: Automating Data Monetization with Integrity

Smart contracts, self-executing pieces of code running on the blockchain, offer an elegant solution to automate and secure data transactions. By encoding the terms and conditions of data usage into smart contracts, businesses can ensure that data is only monetized under predefined conditions. This not only streamlines the monetization process but also mitigates the risks associated with manual transactions.

Blockchain and Data Scoring

- ***Personal data stores***

As individuals interact with numerous organizations online through various digital services, their personal data gets scattered across different databases with little centralized oversight or control. This makes it difficult for individuals to keep track of all the data being collected about them and to exercise their rights like access, correction, or deletion. Personal data stores hosted on blockchain offer a solution by allowing individuals to consolidate all their data in one place.

A personal data store is implemented as a decentralized application on the blockchain. The individual owns a private key that gives them access to write data to and read from their personal data store contract hosted on the blockchain network. All personal data is encrypted, and access is controlled through a private key. The decentralized application allows individuals to import structured and unstructured data about themselves from major data sources like social networks, payment services, IoT devices, etc. through APIs. It standardizes the format to facilitate storage as assets on the blockchain.

Smart contracts enforce individual ownership and control over personal data assets. Individuals have permission to grant temporary access to specific personal attributes to third parties for defined purposes. All access and modifications are recorded immutably on-chain. Personal data stores can be made discoverable on decentralized applications like personal profiles and resumes. Individuals have full control over visibility, and opt-out mechanisms are accessible at any time. However, as adoption increases, standards are being developed for personal data stores. Interoperability across different implementations and the ability to port data assets between blockchain networks will be key drivers for these decentralized personal data ecosystems.

Data rights and portability

Under this field, individuals must be able to easily access and view any and all personal data assets stored within their personal data store. The decentralized application (DApp) interface should allow for simple discovery and retrieval of all data in a human-readable format. Clicking on a specific data asset would reveal its details. The interface could include search capabilities to help locate desired information. If individuals find any inaccurate or outdated personal data upon accessing their store, they must be empowered to request modifications. The DApp should support encryption-protected editing of existing personal data assets directly on the blockchain in a verifiable manner. This ensures only the individual can edit their personal information. Edit requests would initiate encrypted transactions on the blockchain to update relevant assets.

To exercise their right to erasure, individuals must be able to irreversibly delete specific personal data assets within their custody. The data store DApp should facilitate permanent on-chain removal through deletion transactions on the blockchain network. Deletion requests would remove all traces of the specified assets from the individual's store. Interoperability is key to allowing the portable transfer of an individual's consolidated personal data bundle between different personal data store implementations, whether within one blockchain or across heterogeneous networks. Standards are required for standardized data formatting and normalized APIs to power portability. This lets individuals easily switch services while maintaining control over their personal information.

The architecture and features of decentralized personal data stores must comply with all applicable data protection laws and regulations that mandate support for individual data rights. This ensures individuals have seamless control over their personal information, regardless of where it is stored through blockchain-powered personal data stores.

Data scoring algorithms

With personal data consolidated in on-chain stores, algorithms can analyse this information to derive insights about individuals in the form of data scores. Different methodologies exist to calculate these scores based on categories like consumption patterns (purchase history, interests), health indicators (fitness activities, medical records), finances (income, investments) and more. Scoring models employ techniques like predictive analytics, trend analysis, and statistical modelling to combine various personal attributes into composite metric scores.

For scores to be useful and trusted, the algorithms must be explainable by providing transparency into how the ratings are determined. Techniques like model introspection, prototype selection, and accumulated local effects can be used to discern the key attributes and analytical steps that influence an individual's scores. This allows individuals to verify score accuracy, fix any issues with underlying data, and understand how certain behaviours impact their ratings over time. Explainability is vital for building confidence in data driven assessments of individuals

Incentives for data sharing

To incentivize the secure yet beneficial sharing of personal information, mechanisms can reward individuals for responsibly licensing select attributes to qualifying third parties. For example, individuals may get paid in cryptocurrency tokens for sharing health metrics with approved medical researchers or partial purchase histories with targeted advertising vendors. Smart contracts enable algorithmic payment of micro rewards based on data sensitivity, value to the partner, and contractual terms of the sharing agreement.

Beyond direct payment, reputation and credit systems can also incentivize quality data-sharing behaviours. Individual profiles that regularly share accurate attributes with validated partners may receive higher data-driven "reputation scores" over time. Similarly, properly nourishing one's online identity with genuine personal details could improve their "credit scores" which unlock further sharing and monetization opportunities. Such tokenized reputation and credit may even hold broader real-world utility and value in the long run.

Data marketplace frameworks

Blockchain allows for the technical design of peer-to-peer marketplaces where individuals can monetize their personal data assets. Anonymized parts of individuals' consolidated profiles can be tokenized and listed for third parties like advertisers, researchers, or data brokers to browse and bid on using smart contracts. The marketplaces employ crypto-economic mechanisms to facilitate the matching of data supply and demand. Payments are processed, and data access permissions are managed through on-chain transactions, with individual consent enforced at each step.

Just like traditional assets, personal data trading on such marketplaces would be subject to various pricing models and market forces influencing their valuations. Data assets may be valued differently based on their identified sensitivity levels, exclusivity, or utility for specific purposes. Market liquidity, availability of substitutes, and broader macroeconomic indicators could all impact real-time pricing behaviours. Over time, price histories may emerge for standardized personal attribute bundles, reflecting their demand-supply economic characteristics as a new asset class.

Privacy-preserving analytics

Even when personal data is pooled and anonymized into statistical datasets, advanced analytics could potentially expose individuals. Differential privacy is a technique to add controlled random noise to results that individuals cannot distinguish whether their data was included or not. This allows valuable aggregate insights and patterns to be gleaned from datasets, while provably upholding privacy. Differentially private algorithms calibrate the noise based on desired privacy levels and analytics accuracy.

In addition to differential privacy, other multi-party computation techniques also enable privacy-preserving analytics. For example, homomorphic encryption allows analysis of encrypted data without decrypting it first. Distributed methods divide the dataset and analytics tasks across non-colluding servers so no single party learns an individual's raw attributes. Secure multiparty computation takes this further through protocols that do not even reveal intermediate or final results to any party. Combining these state-of-the-art cryptographic algorithms protects individual privacy at scale.

Protocols for consent and access management

For the sharing of personal information to occur legally, verifiable consent needs to be obtained from individuals. Protocols define standards, like JSON data formats, for individuals to cryptographically sign statements of consent to use select attributes only for specified purposes and durations. These signatures are tied to the individual's cryptographic identity, securely authorizing the use of sensitive personal information for agreed-upon terms.

Corresponding mechanisms allow businesses seeking to access consented personal attributes to cryptographically verify the validity and scope of previously granted approvals. Through zero-knowledge proofs, a business can confirm an individual consented to share attributes X, Y, and Z only until date D without learning the actual attribute values. If actual access is then required, separate encrypted requests are routed through anonymity-preserving systems like mixed networks. This enforces privacy-safe consent-based sharing of sensitive personal information. **Data Valuation**

Sensitive vs non-sensitive data

To appropriately value different types of personal data, a key step involves categorizing information based on sensitivity. Data relating to finances, government IDs, health status, and unique biometric attributes are typically deemed highly sensitive. Demographic facts, consumer preferences, and online activities are moderately sensitive. Publicly shared names, photos, and casual location check-ins have relatively low sensitivity. Methods analyse attribute details as well as re-identification risks to assess inherent sensitivities.

Multiple factors determine an attribute's sensitivity beyond its natural classification. For example, health details are more sensitive if they are precisely time-stamped than generalized symptoms. Locations exposing private routines are more sensitive than popular landmarks. Aggregate behavioural datasets revealing routines are more sensitive than anonymous samples. The intended context, extent of other known attributes, and potential misuse all influence sensitivity beyond basic categories. This nuanced understanding ensures personal data is responsibly valued relative to actual privacy risks.

Data attribute scoring

To systematically value personal data attributes, scoring approaches assign weighted metrics based on sensitivity analysis and other risk-related factors. Attributes deemed highly sensitive are given high scores proportional to their perceived risks and potential harms. Factors like attribute uniqueness/rarity also influence scores since less common details heighten re-identifiability.

Identifiable risks corresponding to known attribute linkages similarly impact scores. The assigned scores capture holistic risks and serve as common units for valuation comparisons.

Attribute scores result from factoring in multiple considerations rather than a single category. While health records have intrinsic sensitivity, precautions like generalizing detail and disassociating timestamps could lower their scores. Common location check-ins may not be very sensitive individually but reveal more as a collated set, increasing scores. Data gets re-identified as public records evolve, requiring dynamic scoring. Context also matters - sensitive attributes shared intentionally under strict access protocols may warrant lower short-term monetization scores than passive background inferences. Nuanced attribution models are thus vital for precisely scoring-based valuations.

Consumer surveys on valuation

Several studies have leveraged opinion surveys to understand how much individuals value various personal data attributes and transactions. For example, some surveys presented hypothetical scenarios where respondents had to choose between transactions involving health, financial, or location data to derive relative values. Other conjoint analyses combined attributes into profiles to understand trade-offs. While not direct measures, such surveys provide initial demand-side indications to help benchmark valuations.

However, survey findings also have limitations since opinions do not always translate to real behaviour and choices. Stated preferences on sensitive topics are subject to biases like hyperbolic discounting of long-term risks. Hypothetical scenarios may not reflect complex real-world conditions influencing decisions. Also, perceptions change rapidly as technologies evolve and public understanding grows. While useful for qualitative trends, survey data needs other context factors to determine quantitative benchmarks for personal data valuation models. Guidelines are evolving on survey design best practices to minimize gaps between stated and revealed preferences.

Value of consented data sharing

As personal data marketplaces emerge, various mechanisms can be used to discover the potential value of attributes that individuals consent to sharing or licensing for approved uses. Auction models allow buyers to bid on tokenized datasets, with clearing prices indicating values in competitive scenarios. Dynamic pricing algorithms also adjust suggested prices in real time based on supply and demand schedules to find market equilibrium values. Both approaches factor in usage contexts pre-defined by individual consent agreements. Over time, value benchmarks may be learned for different attribute classes and sharing agreements.

While useful to gauge market-driven values, such techniques also require adjusting for contextual consent-based restrictions that may lower practical monetization potential. For example, licensing attributes purely for non-commercial research may garner less value than profiles optimized for targeted advertising. Similarly, short-term access consented under rigid protocols limits ongoing monetization avenues compared to perpetual undefined use. Consent and usage context are thus important prisms through which to interpret value signals from auction and pricing mechanisms for ethically sharing personal information markets.

Value of aggregated anonymized data

To determine the monetary worth of pooled and anonymized statistical datasets containing personal information, analytical techniques can be applied. The value is often correlated with the overall sample size and the richness of attributes included after anonymization transformations. However, successive reductions in identifiable traits render the data progressively less useful and, hence, less valuable to potential buyers. Formal risk-utility frameworks allow the modelling of this decreasing marginal value with weaker anonymization.

For example, datasets with full postal codes remain more valuable than those with just state-level locations. General age ranges retain more value than just broad age brackets. Omitting rare attributes preserves uniqueness better. With each step of ambiguity, actionable insights and monetization opportunities diminish according to protected risks. This allows quantification of anonymity's effect on demand schedules and price points for aggregated data assets. Combined with consent and legal compliance, it ensures data is rightly valued per privacy expectations.

Data derivatives and risk factors

Personal data valuation models need to account for external risks that can decrease an asset's worth over time. Uncontrolled data breaches by third parties pose severe reputational and financial risks. Loss of access due to compromised policies also reduces demand. Quantifying historical breach frequencies, outcomes, and their probability allows for adjusting valuations downward accordingly. Provisions for potential liability claims further influence risk-adjusted pricing. Valuers thus discount intrinsic attribute values based on contextualized breach exposures.

At the same time, aggregated and anonymized datasets used to produce valuable derivatives like metrics and analytics have commercial worth that is independent of the source of personal information.

For example, real-time influenza spread indicators or demographic trend forecasts. These derived works growing out of personal data may therefore earn separate value streams beyond their original assets. Models aim to fairly attribute such value gains across contributors, acknowledging that data is an input as well as an asset in its own right. Partitioning worth by risk and derivative factors captures full economic characteristics.

Transaction cost implications

A full valuation of personal data assets must consider the various transaction costs incurred in the acquisition, exchange, and verification of data. Costs like identifier resolution, profiling, consent management, and privacy-preserving delivery all represent overheads that impact the net realizable value market places. Normalizing data formats, performing integrity checks, and documenting transactions also involve expenditures. These real-world costs of finding buyers, negotiating terms, and fulfilling orders shape the breakeven price points.

Factors like average processing speeds, success rates, and fulfilment margins determine the viable operating expenses that further reduce realizable valuations below theoretical estimates. Monitoring technical, financial, and contractual performance metrics helps determine relative efficiencies across platforms and methods over time. Only through understanding the complete cost structure influencing supply chain activities can accurate price discovery and benchmarks for personal information assets be established to drive efficient privacy-friendly markets.

Total data value accounting

To fully recognize the strategic importance and economic value of personal data, frameworks are needed for businesses to comprehensively account for their proprietary and contracted data assets on balance sheets. This involves valuing direct sources like first-party customer profiles as well as derived assets like ML models and identities. Indirect sources through data partnerships are also included. Values are determined through appropriate techniques adjusted for consent, risk, and costs. Regular revaluations factor in market and technological changes.

Quantifying total data value positions companies to optimize governance and monetization strategies. It also requires supplementary reporting mechanisms beyond traditional ledgers to disclose components transparently. Disaggregating figures by attribute types, consents, usage contexts, and risk factors shows analytic rigor and compliance. Over time, standardized schemas may emerge for businesses across sectors to adopt for credible valuation-based data management and auditing. This establishes personal information as a traceable corporate asset class, supporting stewardship.

Data valuation standards

As data-driven business models proliferate and data sharing becomes more prevalent, standardized valuation frameworks are crucial for transparency, accountability, and fair exchange. Multiple stakeholders are working to develop common standards, reference models, taxonomies, and audit protocols. This involves principles for respecting individual privacy and consent throughout the valuation process. Agreeing on core methodologies, metrics, and terminology will promote consistent, credible, and comparable valuation practices.

Leading standards development organizations are engaged in efforts to provide scalable yet rigorous valuation guidance. This builds on ongoing work framing privacy, data quality, and metadata requirements. Emerging guidelines focus on method selection based on attribute sensitivities, risk, and economic factors. They establish documentation duties and promote the assurance of algorithmic valuations. Over time, voluntary standards will ideally evolve into global industry specifications, incorporating lessons from early implementation projects across national and regional data marketplace initiatives.

Applying Blockchain to Data Privacy and Monetization:

Several innovative frameworks leverage blockchain's properties to address the data privacy and monetization challenges. Here are some promising approaches:

Self-Sovereign Identity (SSI): Individuals hold and manage their identity data, granting access to specific information to authorized parties, and empowering them to control their data footprint. Self-Sovereign Identity (SSI) is a new way to manage digital identities that gives individuals more control over their identity data. SSI allows individuals to create and manage their own digital identities, rather than relying on centralized authorities like governments or corporations. This means that people can decide who they share their identity information with, and have more privacy and security.

SSI is based on the idea of decentralized Identifiers (DIDs), which are unique identifiers that are not controlled by any central authority. DIDs are typically stored on a blockchain, which makes them tamper-proof and easy to verify.

With SSI, individuals can use their DIDs to create and manage their own digital identities. They can add attributes to their identities, such as their name, age, and address. They can also create different identities for different purposes, such as a professional identity and a personal identity.

Although SSI is still in its early stages of development, it has the potential to revolutionize the way we manage our digital identities.

Data Marketplaces: Decentralized platforms empower users to independently sell their data to interested parties while maintaining control and transparency over the transaction, including setting their own terms and conditions. Data marketplaces are platforms that facilitate the buying and selling of data. They offer a means for data owners to benefit from their data and for data buyers to access the data they require. These marketplaces can be used to trade various types of data, including personal data, business data, and public data.

As businesses increasingly recognize the value of data, data marketplaces are becoming more popular. They offer a convenient and efficient way for businesses to buy and sell data, which can help them enhance their decision-making and operations.

Tokenized Data: Tokenization is a process that involves converting an asset into a digital token that can be traded on a blockchain network. This process breaks down the asset into smaller, more manageable units, each of which is represented by a unique token. These tokens can be bought, sold, or traded on a decentralized exchange, providing greater liquidity and transparency than traditional asset markets.

Tokenization offers several advantages over traditional asset ownership, including increased security, reduced transaction costs, and the ability to fractionalize ownership. By representing assets as digital tokens, it becomes easier to track and manage ownership, reducing the risk of fraud and theft. Additionally, tokenization can enable the creation of new financial products and services, such as tokenized real estate, tokenized art, and tokenized commodities.

Overall, tokenization is a powerful tool that has the potential to revolutionize how we own and trade assets. It provides a secure, efficient, and transparent way to represent and transfer ownership of assets, opening up new possibilities for investment and financial innovation.

Privacy-Enhancing Technologies (PETs): Techniques like homomorphic encryption allow data analysis without revealing its contents, enabling insights and monetization while safeguarding individual privacy.

Privacy-enhancing technologies (PETs) are a collection of tools and techniques used to safeguard the privacy of individuals and organizations. These technologies work by reducing the amount of personal data that is collected, stored, and processed, and by ensuring that the data is used only for authorized purposes.

PETs can be used to protect data in a variety of settings, including:

Online: PETs can be used to protect data that is collected and stored online, such as personal information, financial information, and health information.

Offline: PETs can be used to protect data that is stored offline, such as paper records and electronic files.

In transit: PETs can be used to protect data that is transmitted between different locations, such as over the Internet or through the mail.

Some common PETs include:

Encryption: *Encryption is the process of converting data into a form that cannot be easily understood by unauthorized people.*

De-identification: *De-identification is the process of removing personal identifiers from data, such as names, addresses, and phone numbers.*

Pseudonymization: *Pseudonymization is the process of replacing personal identifiers with fictitious identifiers, called pseudonyms.*

PETs are an important tool for protecting privacy in the digital age. They can help to reduce the risk of data breaches, identity theft, and other privacy violations.

Challenges and Considerations:

The potential benefits of blockchain for data privacy and monetization are significant. However, several challenges need to be addressed before blockchain can be widely adopted for these purposes.

While blockchain offers exciting possibilities, several challenges remain:

Scalability: Current blockchain technologies struggle to handle large-scale data transactions, requiring further development and optimization. Scalability refers to the ability of a blockchain network to efficiently and effectively handle a growing number of transactions and users without compromising its performance or security. As blockchain technology gains traction and adoption, the need for scalability becomes increasingly crucial.

Current blockchain platforms, such as Bitcoin and Ethereum, face challenges in achieving scalability. These challenges arise due to inherent limitations in their underlying architectures. For instance, Bitcoin's proof-of-work consensus mechanism, while secure, is computationally intensive and results in slow transaction processing times. Ethereum, on the other hand, employs a proof of-stake consensus mechanism, which offers improved scalability compared to proof-of-work but still faces limitations in handling high transaction volumes.

To address these scalability concerns, researchers, and developers are actively exploring various solutions and approaches. One promising approach is sharding, which involves dividing the blockchain into smaller, more manageable segments called shards. Each shard processes its own transactions independently, reducing the computational burden on the entire network and increasing overall scalability.

Regulations: The legal landscape surrounding data ownership and monetization in a blockchain context is still evolving, requiring clear and adaptable regulations. Regulations play a crucial role in shaping the legal landscape surrounding data ownership and monetization in the context of blockchain technology. As the blockchain industry continues to evolve, clear and adaptable regulations are essential to ensure responsible and ethical practices.

One of the key regulatory considerations is data privacy and protection. Blockchain technology enables the decentralized storage and sharing of data, raising concerns about how personal information is collected, used, and secured. Regulations should address these concerns by establishing data protection standards, ensuring transparency, and providing individuals with control over their data.

User Adoption: Encouraging widespread adoption of new data management practices demands user education and trust-building initiatives. User adoption is a critical factor in the success of any new technology, and blockchain is no exception. For blockchain technology to reach its full potential, users must understand its benefits and be willing to adopt it.

However, despite these challenges, the potential of blockchain for data privacy and monetization is clear. By providing a secure and transparent way to manage data, blockchain can help to create a more equitable and efficient data economy.

CHAPTER EIGHT

THE DEVELOPER'S TAKE ON DATA COMPLIANCE MADE SIMPLE

If you're a small business owner, you probably have a lot on your plate, and navigating the technical aspects of data compliance can seem overwhelming. However, gaining insight from a developer's perspective can help simplify the process. Let's break it down in simple terms.

Understanding Data Compliance: It's a Team Effort

In the digital age, businesses are required to collect and utilize customer information, which comes with certain responsibilities. Data compliance ensures that this information is handled ethically and securely. From the developer's perspective, this involves setting up systems and processes to safeguard customer data. It is a team effort to ensure data compliance.

Why Should You Care?

Imagine that your business is a castle, and the customer data you possess is the treasure inside. To safeguard your treasure from invaders, you need to implement data compliance measures, much like building a moat around your castle. It's not just a legal requirement, it's also good business practice. When your customers feel secure and happy with your services, they are more likely to stay loyal and recommend you to others.

The Developer's Role: Building a Fortified Castle

Encryption

Developers use encryption to turn sensitive information into a secret code. It's like having a treasure chest with a magical lock only you can open. Even if someone tries to snatch the chest, they can't open it without the right key.

Access Controls

Imagine your data as different rooms in a castle, where access controls allow only trusted knights to enter specific rooms, preventing unauthorized access.

Regular Audits

Developers regularly audit your digital defenses to identify any vulnerabilities. They search for cracks or weak spots in your system, ensuring that everything is as secure as it should be. It's similar to having an architect inspect your physical castle to make sure it remains standing tall.

User Permissions

Just as you wouldn't give every castle dweller the same level of access, developers create different roles for users. For instance, your treasurer might have access to the treasury, but the chef doesn't. This minimizes the risk of sensitive information falling into the wrong hands.

Legal Compliance

Data compliance isn't just about protecting your customers; it's also about following the laws of the digital realm. Developers ensure that your business practices align with these laws, avoiding legal battles and ensuring smooth sailing for your kingdom.

Communication: Building Bridges with Transparency

Transparency is key. Developers play a role in making sure you communicate with your customers about how their data is used. It's like putting up signs in your castle, so everyone knows what to expect. Trust is built on openness.

Everyone Plays a Part

In the grand scheme of things, data compliance is a collaborative effort. Developers are like architects and builders, constructing the digital fortress to keep your business safe. But just like in a castle, everyone—from the guards at the gates to the residents inside—has a role in maintaining security.

Come with me as I show you some giant companies that suffered data breaches in recent times:

A data breach occurs when unauthorized individuals gain access to sensitive data, which can result in its unauthorized acquisition, use, disclosure, or loss. This can affect personal information, financial records, intellectual property, and trade secrets. Recent high-profile breaches, including those affecting Uber, Mercedes, and Adobe, emphasize the importance of strong cybersecurity measures and increased awareness of data protection.

Uber

In 2016, Uber, the popular ride-sharing service, experienced a significant data breach that resulted in the personal information of 57 million drivers and users being compromised. The breach occurred when two hackers gained unauthorized access to a private GitHub repository utilized by Uber engineers. The stolen data included sensitive information such as names, email addresses, phone numbers, and driver's license details. Uber faced criticism for not promptly disclosing the breach, and the incident was not made public until 2017. This resulted in legal consequences and a settlement with the Federal Trade Commission (FTC).

Mercedes

In 2021, the luxury car manufacturer Mercedes-Benz suffered a data breach that affected its customers in the United States. The breach was caused by a misconfiguration of cloud storage, which resulted in the exposure of sensitive information such as social security numbers, credit card details, and driver's license information. Mercedes-Benz promptly notified its affected customers and took measures to improve its cybersecurity, but the incident highlighted the vulnerability of even well-established brands to cyber threats.

Adobe

In 2013, Adobe, a well-known software company, faced a major data breach. This breach exposed the personal information of around 38 million users, including encrypted passwords and credit card information. The attackers took advantage of vulnerabilities in Adobe's security systems, highlighting the need for continuous monitoring and prompt mitigation measures. As a result of this incident, Adobe took measures to enhance its security protocols and better protect user data.

Best practices for developing secure code

Coding securely is vital for any business, as it can have a significant impact on:

The revenue and profitability of the company

The loyalty and satisfaction of the customers

Developing secure code is crucial for small businesses, as it directly impacts various aspects like revenue, profitability, and customer satisfaction. Learning from the mistakes of major companies, it's evident that code-related issues can compromise both reputation and security. Here are some practical best practices tailored for small businesses:

Security Frameworks and Libraries:

Secure Coding for Small Businesses

Small businesses can benefit from using security frameworks as a guide, providing a structured approach to coding securely.

Regularly scan project dependencies using tools like OWASP Dependency Check and Retire.JS to detect vulnerabilities in third-party code.

Limit the exposure of libraries by wrapping them, only revealing necessary behaviour within your software.

Secure Database Access

Avoid insecure dynamic queries that use untrusted input. Instead, implement query parameterization to prevent SQL injection attacks.

Follow secure configuration guidelines for databases, avoiding default settings. Refer to resources like the OWASP Database Cheat Sheet.

Ensure secure authentication by authenticating over a secure channel and protecting credentials as outlined in the Database Cheat Sheet.

Encode and Escape Data

Implement output encoding to prevent XSS attacks. Convert special characters into their escape sequences before sending content to the HTML interpreter.

Implement Digital Identity

For small businesses, focus on practical digital identity implementation.

Utilize multi-factor authentication at different levels. Start with strong password policies and, if feasible, explore cryptographic-based authentication for enhanced security.

Properly manage sessions, creating and expiring them appropriately. Consider using tokens like JWT for improved session management.

Ensure All Inputs Are Valid:

Emphasize data validation for small businesses, considering the following concepts:

Syntax and Semantic Validity: Ensure data follows the expected format and meaning rules.

Output Encoding: Encode data appropriately before sending it to target interpreters to prevent potential vulnerabilities. Allow list Validation: Preferentially uses allow list validation, matching data with known good rules, for a more secure approach. By adopting these practices, small businesses can enhance their code security, protecting against potential threats and building trust among customers. Regularly updating knowledge on secure coding practices and staying informed about potential vulnerabilities is also essential for maintaining a secure codebase.

Conclusion: Safeguarding Your Kingdom

Developers must understand the importance of data compliance and take the necessary steps to build a secure environment for customers' information. By collaborating and investing in a robust digital fortress, businesses can meet legal requirements while ensuring customer trust and loyalty. Let your developers be the knights in shining armor, protecting your business kingdom from digital threats.

SUMMARY

In conclusion, it is important to embrace the future and empower your business by adopting responsible data practices. The digital landscape is constantly changing, and it can be overwhelming for small businesses to navigate data privacy regulations. However, this guide has provided you with the knowledge and tools to turn data compliance from a burden into an opportunity.

Embrace Responsibility, Empower Customers

It's essential to understand that data compliance is not just about avoiding fines; it's about building trust with your customers and protecting their privacy. Prioritizing responsible data handling can help you build customer loyalty and gain a competitive edge in a privacy-conscious marketplace.

In the ever-evolving digital landscape, data is the lifeblood of any business, but for small businesses, it can also feel like a ticking time bomb. Navigating the labyrinthine world of data privacy regulations, with its potential fines, reputational damage, and operational hurdles, can leave even the most seasoned entrepreneur feeling overwhelmed. But fear not, intrepid small business owners! You are not alone in this data odyssey.

This comprehensive exploration has illuminated the crucial importance of data compliance for small businesses. We've unveiled the lurking threats, demystified complex regulations, and highlighted the challenges you face in ensuring responsible data handling. Remember, compliance is not just about avoiding penalties; it's about building trust with your customers, protecting their privacy, and fostering a sustainable future for your business.

Your AI Guardian Awaits

The AI Compliance Assistant is more than just a compliance tool; it's a trusted partner in your journey. Its real-time monitoring, insightful reporting, and data optimization capabilities empower you to proactively manage compliance and make informed decisions about your data practices.

Enter the AI Compliance Assistant, your knight in shining armour amidst the data maze. This revolutionary tool, armed with cutting-edge artificial intelligence, transcends the role of a mere compliance watchdog. It becomes your personalized guardian angel, constantly monitoring your data practices, identifying potential pitfalls, and guiding you towards responsible data handling.

Explore the Value Spectrum, Choose Your Path

Whether you choose the essential features of the free version or the robust capabilities of the paid version, tailor your choice to your specific needs and budget. Investing in the AI Assistant ensures that you can navigate the data landscape with confidence.

The Future is Bright, Stay Informed

The world of AI-powered compliance is constantly evolving, offering exciting possibilities such as predictive compliance and explainable AI. Staying informed about these trends allows you to leverage cutting-edge solutions and ensure that your business remains compliant. However, don't forget that high-profile companies have fallen flat into the deep ditches of data breaches, so, as a business owner, you need to stay vigilant and employ all veritable tools to avoid walking in their shoes.

Blockchain: A Glimpse into the Future of Data Ownership

While still in its early stages, blockchain technology has the potential to significantly impact data privacy and ethical monetization. As this technology matures, consider exploring its potential to give your customers greater control over their data and unlock new avenues for responsible data-driven innovation.

Remember, the journey to data compliance is ongoing. However, by embracing responsible data practices, utilizing the power of the AI Assistant, and staying informed about evolving trends, you not only empower your business but also your customers, creating a future where trust, transparency, and innovation thrive together.

Take the first step today and begin your journey towards a data-driven future where your business flourishes alongside the trust and respect of your customers.

www.ingramcontent.com/pod-product-compliance
Lightning Source LLC
Chambersburg PA
CBHW022200160726
48282CB00024B/263
* 9 7 8 8 1 9 5 5 8 0 0 6 4 *